RUA DA FELICIDADE

RUA DA FELICIDADE

Ken Norris

VANCOUVER ▼ NEW STAR BOOKS ▼ 2013

NEW STAR BOOKS LTD.
107 — 3477 Commercial Street, Vancouver, BC V5N 4E8 CANADA
1574 Gulf Road, No. 1517, Point Roberts, WA 98281 USA
www.NewStarBooks.com info@NewStarBooks.com

The publisher acknowledges the support of the Government of Canada through the Canada Council and the Department of Canadian Heritage Canada Book Fund, and the Province of British Columbia through the British Columbia Arts Council and the Book Publishing Tax Credit.

Cover design by Oliver McPartlin
Printed on 100% post-consumer recycled paper
Printed and bound in Canada by Gauvin Press
First published October 2013

Cataloguing information for this book is available from
Library and Archives Canada, www.collectionscanada.gc.ca.

CONTENTS

RUA DA FELICIDADE

Elinor agreed to it all, for she did not think he deserved the compliment of rational opposition.

JANE AUSTEN, *Sense and Sensibility*

Smile, though your heart is aching,
Smile, even though it's breaking.

CHARLIE CHAPLIN, "Smile"

O if I am to have so much, let me have more!

WALT WHITMAN,
"Out Of The Cradle Endlessly Rocking"

Love ate the red wheelbarrow.

JACK SPICER, "A Red Wheelbarrow"

THE IMPOSSIBLE

Getting postcards from the impossible, reading what's written
there
in red and black ink. Posted in a purple envelope, the cards
without stamps or addresses. The Images: a big-mouthed
Martha Raye, with reddest lipstick, shouting
a thin eye-browed forties hello. And, in calmer mode,
two women of Tahiti seated pensively on a broad pandanus
mat,
amidst the tropic colours foreign dreams
and idle thoughts nestled in their heads. On the written sides
the impossible says what it must always say,
in the warmth of its remoteness.

And you will never tire of wanting
what cannot be possessed. The impossible
charms you with its candor, its joy, with its
awe-inspiring across-the-room wave.

Unlike what's possible, the impossible
has no secret intentions. It just smiles
its enigmatic smile and moves on,
head in the clouds,
wearing its yellow shoes.

IMPERMANENCE

Perpetual rain. Now a warmer summer rain.
But don't think that the roof is static
or your identity is fixed. It's all being washed away.

It's all transforming, second to second,
the world is flux, there isn't anything
lasts too long.

                    He's dying,
she's coming into prominence, the wheel
turning once again. It never
stops, you just stop watching it,
your heart in vertigo, your shoes in the quicksand
of everything you could never control.

THE SUMMER SKY

The changeable summer sky.

The blue, blue, blue
of hovering nothingness.

Or the wall of grey cloud
and scent of pelting rain.

Or the jagged lightning-bolt
shattering the skylights
and obliterating the stars.

Summer spreads out its green blanket,
flowers come and go, the lilies now
entrenched and holding.
The usual ant parade unfolding
in the scenic black vista of the driveway.

The drifting summer sky
whispers of infinite things.

CLOUDS

Do the clouds look different to you
now that you too are drifting?

And can you descry
any discernible shapes
out of their pillowy whiteness?

You drift across the skies of the world
looking for a place to land, try to find
a formality that suits you.

You sail the world in your paper boat,
eventually throw out your cordless anchor.

THE BARRIER

The barrier is constructed
of cloud and hems in the day.

It's a wall we can't get across.
It blocks us from the open sky.

Life clapped in irons,
all the citizens rounded up
and put on trains that are going nowhere.

We're stuck here, we're stalled,
we can't get back to the boundless,
can't begin to reach the silver estuary.

AFTER

After ashes,
after the slow settling of the pre-dawn fog,
after hallucinations seen in the red-framed mirror.
After all the green has been leeched out of the landscape,
after shadows have declined,
after the tree has been riven by lightning.

The morning invades with its autumnal chill,
and slowly green flows back
into the trees, bushes, and grass.
Silence hovers over the flowers,
as the brown-eyed susans sway
in the gentleness of a flickering breeze.

THE TURNING

You reach for the form
you cannot find.
It has vanished.

The form you followed,
the form you knew so well.

Knew so well it even had a name,
sometimes a face.

You'll have to go on
without it now.
You'll have to make your own way.

ITINERARIES

I was always heading off to distant lands.

In search, of beauty mostly.

The half-clad sylphlike wahine
rising out of Pacific sea-spray,
or the round-faced oriental with almond eyes
descending out of a Southeast Asian sky.

Oh, there was so much to see:
the Bora Bora lagoon,
the firewalkers of Mbennga,
mid-ocean coral reefs,
the restored ruins of Europe,
the toppled jungle ruins of Khmer temples,
Tibetan refugees
in the villages around Kathmandu,
the emerald Buddha,
the multiple Buddhas of Borobodur
going in and out of reality.

I fell in love with so many places —
Fiji, Tahiti, Prague, Phuket, Santiago, Phnom Penh —
and the names of women would adorn
the places that touched my heart.

And there were the selves inside me I didn't know.

That emerged in those foreign lands.

PRAYER WHEELS

The open sky over Kathmandu,
and rich incense burning at ground level.
Untethered cattle wander
the labyrinthine medieval streets.

The air smells
of hashish
and incense
and cow dung
and urine.

That unique air of Kathmandu.

And I'm wanting all the Nepalis
serving in the restaurants
to know I am not an Israeli —
otherwise
they'll spit in my food.

The air itself
is light with altitude
and Hinduism.
Everywhere I go
my eyes are attacked
by colours and prayer flags.

Up on the rooftop
of the rickety hotel
I'm looking out over
the Kathmandu valley,
admiring the mountains.

Climbing up to the top
of the Monkey Temple,
I spin the prayer wheels.
As the monkeys look on, my aspirations
take to the sky.

GHOSTS

The girl who jumped from the Vancouver Island ferry.
The woman who held a falling man's jacket for three days.

They lie down beside me as I sleep.
Sad ghosts who cannot find peace.

THE YOUNG

They come to see me
with their sorrows, their difficulties,
their broken links
and fractured hearts.

They want answers and solutions,
balms and bandages.

I'm old and wise, you see.
I've been around the block.

They struggle with everything:
struggle to find balance,
struggle to make the rent,
struggle to understand.

I smile, comfort them,
dig down deep
in my bag of experience
to find something
I think they can use.

When I have something I offer it,
and they walk away,
temporarily relieved,
mollified.

The young suffer so much.
It is so easy to be young.

DULUTH EAST

I walk past that street
with more than a little sadness.
All the mayhem that was to follow
started in that calm apartment
above the Portuguese café.

My very adult life
began there, and who could know
how it would all turn out?

That was twenty years ago.
I met her, and fell in love.
In a snowstorm
we moved all our possessions in
by taxi.

We didn't have much,
and all that mattered then was the bed,
a sacred place to lie down and love.

ADDRESSES

I only have memories of streets and avenues:
Prince Arthur, Hampton,
Aylmer, Clark, Duluth,
Hôtel de Ville.

Only in a few cases
can I even find the houses —
the one on Aylmer
is falling down and has been condemned,
the one on Prince Arthur
still identifiable by its corner location.

But I'm losing specific sense
of where I lived,
and the memories are going.

Who lives there now,
and what lives and loves
do they embrace?

It's difficult to come back
and not remember,
difficult to have been replaced.

If I were lost
and drunk in a taxi
I could not get home
to any of you.

All the numbers have faded.

THE END OF THE DAY

The mind begins to cascade
at the end of the day.

It can't attach its hooks
to the real.

It just slides off
wanting sleep.

I've run it around
through the green rigours of daylight,

and now it wants to commune
with a sky full of stars.

Though it can't comprehend them
as they flicker there in the baffling dark.

VARIOUS THINGS

I'll pull together the catalogue
of various things, a miscellany
of this and that, exercise my being.

Walk the paths of the world.
I'll wave hello to strangers,
and move along.

I never stay long
in any one condition.
I get restless, you see.

I move from point to point,
feel loss every time.
I must depart.

Gather new specimens
for my burgeoning catalogue
of various things.

OLD ENEMIES

I don't pay them any mind.
I just let them disappear.

Time drops by
and carries them off,
and their tedious works
are carried off with them, flailing.

The eighteenth century
didn't need to be reprised
after all.

Oh, they were a band
of formal fellows,
and their formality
almost touched me.

But life and art
are about more than etiquette,
and when permitted
to be themselves
they exhibited
venal tendencies
and abysmal manners.

DENSITY

Sunlight's thick as honey,
pouring down
out of that slow placid sky.

And all the spaces
between atoms
compress.

Density.

I'll go out wandering
under a hot sun
that draws out my sweat.

And the heat will weaken the asphalt,
a few small bridges will collapse,
a tornado will touch down
somewhere in the vicinity
of whatever's wild and going on.

The shallow lake

lifted.

TALK

It is good to talk
late into the night
unraveling secrets and concerns.

Things need to be said,
to be exhumed, dragged out
into the light and placed
on the kitchen table for inspection.

Otherwise, how do we know ourselves?
And how can we ever understand what has happened?

So friends talk late
into the night, infrequently,
but with a necessity
that pours out
straight from the roots of being.

Those we loved
are loved again, their names
uttered with reverence,
their lost presences
felt inside the room.

CHANGES

Morning fog shifts over the quiet river,
the green trees register their autumnal changes.
It's the last of summer, and I have arrived.
Arrived at the grass and rolling hills,
of the last days of summer.

When summer ends I'll go to a foreign land
where the seasons will be different
and I will enter the different days differently.
I'll walk the hot streets of Asia,
a large portion of my days behind me.

Though early, already traffic's
streaming across the bridge, people
being purposeful, on their way to work.
This is my work, standing by the window
watching the fog float over the river, slowly
feeling everything change.

All the industry of the city grows quiet —
in respect of the sun going down.
Golden light grazes the skyscrapers,
painted Skytrains go by.

I used to see clouds like that
in Japanese paintings.

And now the whole city is busy
praising the gods.
Across the way the yellow derricks
stand idle. All the workers
have gone home.

They'll put up that building
day by day
until one day
it's just standing there,
part of the urban landscape.

Pale blue clouds in a pale blue sky.
The sun now kissing the Amari Boulevard Hotel.

STREETS OF BANGKOK

I wander the streets of Bangkok
looking for old loves.

Everywhere there is hammering,
the city being rebuilt,
and the traffic
sludgy and aggressive.

If I say their names out loud
I will lose them forever.

So I wander the night market,
go past the streetside restaurant
where the tall one and I used to eat
as the traffic poured by
and the nighttime swallowed up our laughter.

And I walk past the tuk-tuk driver
who, though slightly older,
still recognizes me
from the nights the small one and I
hired his services
to transport us to our magical abode.

Now Muslim women
are shuffling in the streets,

moving through the night market dressed all in black,
an oppressive sadness in their eyes and faces.

Bangkok is changing.
What lives they live
with their strict husbands
and chains of customs I'll never know.

I miss them,
the tall one, the small one.

If I say their names out loud
without seeing their faces
I will lose them both forever.

YELLOW CURRY

It stands
at the apex of sublimity.

And where do they get
those potatoes,
so rich in intriguing flavour?
They are a challenge
to anyone who ever might say
potatoes are bland.

This curry
honours the chicken
that died to anchor it,
it gives chunks of pellucid onion
pride of place.

Oh, praise be to the cook
who works diligently
preparing this textured feast.

And a deep bow
to the steamed white rice
that soaks up the curry sauce.

UNTAMED HORSE

for Zoe

You're going to have to learn
how to ride
that untamed horse.

How to control it,
how to concentrate its energies.

The horse is wild
and wants to go
where it wants to go.

Most of all
it wants its freedom.

It's willing to carry you off
to the far distances,
or else throw you off entirely.

It's the horse you've been given.
You must learn to tame it,
the horse that is your own.

THE OLD ROAD

The old road is congested.

The old road winds too far
and takes too long.

The old road may be colourful,
but it's a hassle.

You spend extra hours
wondering if you'll be crushed.

The old road may have been good enough
for someone's grandfather,

but your father certainly didn't like it,
and, henceforth, you'll refuse to take it.

THE MAN IN THE ROOM

The man in the room with the green tropics all around him
is slowly creating his counterlife.

This one.
This life in art.

The life in the room
that is the imagination.

He asks the landscape
to welcome him in.

He wants the trees
to know him.

Travels deeper and deeper
into the painting on the wall.

It's a muggy day in an Asian city,
all the pleasure to be found is inside.

He sits at a writing desk,
under the air conditioner.

The desk has magically appeared.
As has his laundry.

So he drinks water
and writes.

A poem so intimate
he dissolves

into the ink
and the paper.

STEAMY

The warm morning rain turns to steaminess,
and now the city exudes a jungle heat,
and one staggers along the crowd-thronged streets
not knowing where anyone is going
or, in fact, what anything means.

The steaminess gets to you,
this is how the gutted dead fish must feel
if they still can feel, as the steam
rises, cooking them.

On days like this in Bangkok
the air is close, and fetid,
and the steaminess of the city
takes the purpose right out of you.

The clouded sky closes over everything
like a coffin-lid, like the lid
of the pot the fish are steamed in,
and everyone moves about listlessly
in the torpor of dying to be alive.

NEWS OF DEATH

It was coming,
we all knew that it was coming.

But now he's gone.

Done dying, gone forever.

And I hear about it
half a world away.

Someone whispers
he has left us.

As someone whispers
of us all.

ONE EVENING IN BATAM

She was a thin Indonesian woman
of indeterminate age,
squatting there in the street,
with great dignity
meticulously going through
the plastic bags of garbage
that had been put out
by the businesses,
looking for something to eat.

I gave her some money.
I should have called her mother
and given her everything I own

SADNESS

There's sadness in the rain,
there's sadness in the blue
of the sky.

And sadness is a weight
borne by all beings.

We meet, only to depart
in sadness.

As our friend
is lowered into the ground
we feel the weight
everywhere around and within us.

Now make a case for happiness.

INA

She can't take the compliment
when I praise her beauty,
my line of artful discourse
won't get me anywhere with her.

If I could say it in Bahasa
maybe it would take,
and my silver tongue
would get me deeper
into her consciousness.

But I say it in English,
and no matter how artfully
I put it, it's in
a foreign language
she's just browsing for information.

SINGAPORE

The Chinese women and their multi-coloured sun umbrellas.
They're trying to keep their skin as white as possible.

On the MRT
it's a very British pre-recorded voice
announcing the station stops.

The official language is English
but no one seems to speak it.
I hear Mandarin, Hindi, Cantonese, Bahasa Indonesian,
   Arabic.
In every part of the city.

The sun beats down on steamy Singapore
as everyone attempts to hold their ground.

HEAVY AIR

It's a day of heavy air,
the pallid sky pressing down.

Roosters and chickens in the back lane
peck about the gravel, humans
wander aimlessly, or sit in doorways,
or conclude a long day of disappointing business,
going home to unsatisfactory houses.

It's a day that brings
everyone's impatience to the surface,
that litters the world with crows
and red rooftiles, entirely missing
the drama of the monsoon rains.

THOSE DAYS

The winds of the North and South
left me a little westerly,
and so those days passed by.
Everything was at sea.

Without a doubt, I earned the title
of wandering vagabond.
I wore every kind of hat,
I knew fast women;
I ate sand, I ate salmon,
and I married from time to time.

But without presuming to be
emperor or sailor,
I must tell you I remember
the most amiable hurricanes,
and that now I die of envy
remembering what I no longer have:
the riches that I had and didn't have,
the hunger that kept me running,
and those intrusive husband's shoes
that never kicked in the door.

What is great about joy
is the doubled self it has.
And one doesn't live in today alone —
the present is a suitcase

with a hot watch inside.
Our hearts court the future
and our pleasures are long gone.

And so I rambled from road to road,
in heat, in cold, and in haste,
and all I didn't see
I'm still remembering now —
all the shadows I swam in,
every ocean that received me.
I rapped out a beat on all the stones,
I lay down with the thorns,
and I had the natural honour
of those not born to privilege.

I don't know why I'm telling you all these things —
these sites, these moments,
this smoke from all those lost bonfires.
No one thinks it's important
to tremble with the earthquake survivors,
and, truly, no one cares
about anyone else's youth.
So I'm not asking you to pardon me.
And I am where I always am.
I have a tree with so many leaves
that, although I don't lay any claim to immortality,
I can laugh at you, and at the autumn.

after Neruda

THE WORK

The work gets done somehow.
I look out the window,
I wander in the streets.

It's a serious mission
of paying attention
to what's going on.

I honour the flowers
and try to ignore the rats.

But you can't ignore them
for very long.

So I go looking
in the night market
for something useful.

THURSDAY

There's incense burning,
and jasmine on the shrines.

And the sun beats down
on Bangkok,
fashioning the day
into something malleable.

The hard count
of minutes
melts away,
effortlessly we enter
the drift of time.

As the smoke
of the burning incense sticks
rises to the sky.

JINGLE

I've got a mind
full of hippo dung.

The day mounts
its campaign.
and I refuse
to vote for it.

I'm stuck
in the crevasses
of absences.

Stray coins
from distant lands
jingle in my pocket.

MISSED IT BY A FRACTION

The perfect life,
perfect moment,
perfect love.

I did miss them all
by a fraction.

Lining up the pool shot,
I barely missed it
because of
overcompensation.

What always
tipped it away
from perfection
was the uncalculated
weight of the mind.

TO A FRIEND

All applause is empty,
so why chase it?

You'd do better
listening to the rain.

SILENCE

Sometimes silence descends like a morning mist.

And it becomes the atmosphere,
the texture of everything.

A deep wordlessness,
an end to words.

And there is only
the quiet moment,
the allness of everything felt
and not uttered.

IT

It wasn't worth
the paper it was printed on.

Maybe it was.
Perhaps it is.

The counterfeit versus the true.

It's an interesting wrestling match,
and not too many
want to take it up.

Like the carpet,
it's too much trouble.

So *carpe diem*
and see you later.

OLD LOVE

I've held her so close
as a perfect memory.

I would have died on this mountain.
For this mountain.

BLUE SKY

You can make no possession
of the blue sky.

You can't put it in your pocket.

We should be grateful for that,
those of us who love the sky.

Those of us who have
always loved the sky,
when we were denied the possibility
of loving anything else.

Nothing lands.

It's all up in the air,
the mandate of projects
unfulfilled.

Every motion
lacks completion.

RIVER SONG

They all flow past —
the Stillwater, the Hudson, the Danube, the Singapore, the
Mekong —
they all flow down to the sea.

Water moves from the mountains
or the hills down
to the lower elevations.

The meandering stories that wind through lives.

Clear placid rivers, or rushing rivers,
or rivers slow and brown
with the silt of centuries.

We watch the boats go by,
or else float on boats
out in mid-river.

The Tonle Sap, the Chao Phraya.

Have a conversation
with the ferryman
or the river merchant's wife,
feel the tug of tide
and pull of eternity.

All flows past,
all flows down to the sea.

PRESENT

The mind veers and swerves
through all the accidents of life,
everything that happened,
everything that might stand to happen.

The past is gone,
and the future
may never arrive.

The only thing
that's vaguely happening
is the rain.

UNTITLED

Ceasing to be.

We have to prepare for it,
have to prepare
for an eternity of not existing.

For all we know is existence.

Where were we
before we existed?
Where will we be
after we've ceased to exist?

DARKNESS

I'm trying to dissuade the darkness
from claiming me.
I'm trying to get it interested
in other things.

I say, Darkness,
collect stamps, go on
a long vacation,
learn to cook,
don't trouble me.

AUTOBIOGRAPHY

I was a snail
keeping to the details,
I was a bird
in perpetual flight.

The human world
rattled me,
but why was that?

It was my first life.
I'd just incarnated down
from the angelic realm.

So the ways of old souls
stumped me.

I was a wave
whose time had not yet arrived,
I was a harbinger
of the changes to come.

I was mystified
by socks and artichokes,
and I spent too much time
staring at the stars.

ONE OF THESE DAYS

One of these days
I'm going to get down to business.
One of these days
I'm going to take you on.

But not now.
It's too early
and I'm too lazy.
I'm walking around
on an indolent island.

Armies upset me.
I have no time
for strategies and battle plans.

But be sure of this —
you're going to hear from me,
and then your walls
will come tumbling down.
One of these days.

HOW IT GOES

I sleep in shallow water,
I drown in a profusion of dreams.

Everywhere I go
I am the stranger
someone thinks he knows.

All of the twisting green
goes winding towards the sky,
all of the ponderous rain
comes pouring down.

I'm dressed in a tuxedo
but the wedding isn't happening.
It happened yesterday,
or will be happening tomorrow.

The fish are laughing
in the river, the birds
are about to fall out of the trees
from exhaustion.

At two in the morning
the moon puts out
its Do Not Disturb sign.

Somewhere down the hall a broom topples over.
Somewhere down the hall someone is falling in love.

ROOF

It doesn't affect you
when it's over there,
when lightning strikes
your neighbour's roof.

Maybe you feel a little sad for them.

But when your own roof falls in

you're in the middle
of a catastrophe,
trying to rescue
whomever you can.

WORKS AND DAYS

I chisel away
the dross, to arrive
at the statue
inside the stone.

Don't be ridiculous.
I make what I can
out of my works and days.

So much of it is luck.

That friend lucky in love,
that other friend lucky in fortune.

The unlucky ones
already gone.

PEDRO'S GONE

They've robbed me
of the pleasure
of watching him pitch.

There was always something
quite sublime
in the way
he structured a game.

Cut fastball, curveball, change-up,
slider, but in
what order?

The beauty of watching
the infinite variations
running counter-intuitive.

And the batters
shaking their heads
walking away.

TSUNAMI

I once marveled
at the Andaman Sea.
And will again,
when calm and order
have been restored.

You don't want to be
in the right place
at the wrong time.

CHANGING THE LANGUAGE

When Zoe was little
she'd drop the "a"
so that the game
we were playing
became Peek Boo.

I was also fond
of how, if something
was all right with her
she'd say "Okay,"
and if it wasn't
she'd say "Nokay."

She has never been afraid
of changing the language.

PUSHING AGAINST THE FORM

We were always at our best
when we were pushing against the form.

And those others?
They were just trying to serve it.

Tying tidy knots, uncomplicated bows.

But we knew how to get our hands greasy,
how to get down in the connection.

Even now, I keep on
tangling with these wires.

And when we pushed against the form
it pushed back.
So we pushed
again and again
until it yielded.

SHIPPING IT OUT

On the boat to Malaga,
on the helicopter to Banda Aceh.

Goods, services, and oddments.

The usual allusions to Spring.

Spring's gone, and it's never returning.
Summer too.

I'll leave it all in my will
to the ones who come after.

They'll need it.
It will be in short supply.

HERE

I loved what I loved,
and lived what I lived,
and never did bother much
to sort it all into categories.

You can separate
this from that,
but why bother?
Eventually, the English
learn to love the French,
and we inhabit one world
where it is everything all together.

ROOFTOPS

Up with the birds
overlooking the rooftops of the world.

Standing on that rooftop
looking out on the bluish mountains
surrounding Kathmandu.

I don't know where I am.
Yes I do. I'm up on a rooftop
in Queens, it's summer,
we're talking, and I'm hoping
you'll fuck me right here
and leave your husband.

And now love is gone
and there are only
these ugly satellite dishes,
bringing in the signals.

When I was a child
we used to play up
on the rooftops.
Only occasionally
did anyone fall.
Mostly balls were lost
in the streets below,
the tar under our feet

threatening to melt
if it was the height of summer.

Buildings were built
so rooftops could exist,
so that lovers had a place to meet,
children had a place to play,
pigeons had a place to land.

FIVE A.M.

I find the first light comforting,
but it isn't here yet.
The night goes on, night
of broken dreams and weird
Odyssean wanderings.
You dream and dream, yet
you never dream your way
back to Ithaka.

First rip in the fabric
of night. Morning
bleeds through.

BANDA ACEH

When everything
has been taken
from you,

everyone you love,
your life,
your livelihood,

what else
are you
left with?

It's back to praying
in the only mosque
left standing.

THE MIDDLE

When you reach the middle
it is actually closer to the end.
Don't ask me why it's so.
I'll just say, "One
of life's mysteries."

But you see the seam
and the way the whole thing
was constructed, though
no one ever tells you
how or why.

So you are in the middle
(which is closer to the end),
you understand how it's built
even if you can't say why,
and someone steps forward
to offer you a smile.

You had better accept it.
It is actually
what you came for.

STYLISTICS

I liked the way
I got comfortable
with that previous style.

And, really,
it wasn't comfort,
it was something else.

It just felt right
for a while, like I knew
what I was doing

and could do it,
could execute
the play.

And today?
Well, it feels
like that style

spit me out,
like I've been
disgorged

from the
belly
of a whale.

BEAUTY

There was beauty,
and it was in transition.

It was happening,
but it wasn't going to last.

We saw it.
While it was there,
before it changed,
before it faded.

SLOUCHING TOWARDS BETHLEHEM

It's the insane fanatic world
Yeats spoke of.
It has arrived.

We'll live with it,
trying not to step
in the puddles of blood.

TWENTY-FIRST CENTURY

It's the twenty-first century
and everything is unreasonable.

You can't reason with anyone,
and logic is a dead art.

Everyone wants to tell you about
how they're feeling,
and why they have good reasons
for doing the terrible things they do.

GIRL WITH AMNESIA

She appears to be about ten years old.
Blonde hair, blue eyes, possibly Scandinavian.
Scrapes on her nose and under her eyebrows,
one little beaded braid in front,
two plastic red beads bracketing a clear one.
Unsmiling, she stares vacantly into the camera.

She's on the front page
of the *Bangkok Post* today (January 15, 2005),
the caption "Little Girl Lost And Lonely."
She's at a hospital in Phuket province,
and it's thought that she lost
both parents in the tsunami waves
of December 26th.
She doesn't know who she is.
She cannot remember anything.

Who would want to remember?

Her picture is in the paper
because the hospital staff is hoping
someone might recognize her.

Recognize that sad face and those lost blue eyes.

She looks a lot like my daughter
when she was that age.

CLOUDY

Has the sky ever been so cloudy?
There's nothing up there but cloud,
no suggestion of blue.

It's a day walled off
from the universe —at night
you can't see the stars or the moon.

So here we are
in the horizontal world,
where all we have is each other.

THAT WOMAN SURVIVOR IN SOUTHERN INDIA, WHO GAVE BIRTH UP ON A HILL

After all that
I couldn't name my newborn
Tsunami.
That takes guts.

LETTERS HOME

Out there in the South Seas
I was always working on my letters home.

Ten page letters to a lover
I was trying to get to stick around.

Eight page letters to a friend
in which I'd try to capture
the sea and the green atmosphere.

All written by hand
in time and with labour.

Those were the good old days,
and they pained me.

I was so far away,
and letters took so long,
so long to reach me,
so long to respond to,
so long to return.

But I was deeply involved
in the paper and the ink,
in the stamps and envelopes,
in the shaping of words,
the formulation of sentiments,

the arduous task
of writing persuasively of love.

HAUNTED BY THE BOOKS I'VE WRITTEN

I suppose I could go back
and read them all
to rediscover all the people that I've been.

Some selves I liked better
than others, but how
I feel about that
all depends
on who I'm being now.

I like the South Seas wanderer now.
I can relate
to how lost he was,
and how he felt
himself to be
an antique slave to beauty.

EAST ASIA HOTEL

Room 612.
Out my window
I can see the Chinese boats
at anchor in Inner Harbour,
and beyond them those persuasive lights
of Mainland China.

Sitting at a table
on a low Chinese stool,
writing words in yellow light,
a poet in East Asia.

Downstairs
from time to time
there are even
a few girls in the lobby.

Seven o'clock,
and the Asian night
pours down.

RUA DA FELICIDADE

Walking down Rua da Caldeira,
on my way to the Street of Happiness.

Rua da Felicidade.
These narrow two blocks
were the hub of the infamous
Macau red-light district
back in the twenties and thirties, and after.
It's hard to believe
that all that fabled wickedness
radiated out from here,
this short street where one now finds
a few Chinese restaurants,
a few red-doored dwellings
inhabited by elderly Chinese
(when they were young
what did they see, what did they do?)
and a whole raft of bakeries and sweet shops.
Cookies and sweets having replaced
who knows what lost sweetnesses?

Friends, it's a surprise
to all of us
that this book could possibly end
on the Street of Happiness.

MORNING IN MACAU

Morning fog slowly lifting off of Inner Harbour,
the small boats traveling out to the larger ones at anchor.
It's still a world of commerce and shipping.

When the fog lifts, what will I see?
The world in its fuller dimension perhaps,
what was always there, the beauty
that couldn't be exploited for profit or gain.

What the rusted tin roofs of the harbour
could tell you about love.

WHERE IT STARTS

The world keeps permutating
and every permutation gets uglier.

So now I know why all the old men
were always walking around shaking their heads.

They'd known a beautiful world
and it up and died on them.

We don't realize how much the death of beauty affects us.
Until we can't find it anymore.

THE ARRANGEMENT

Big orchestrations,
grand pronouncements,
autumn testaments:
they were never my style.

I'll raise my children,
write my poems,
teach my classes,
listen to the music when it's audible,
detail the landscape when it's visible,
touch beauty when beauty
allows me to touch it.

When the teams head north
I'll watch the baseball season unfold
one game at a time,
talking with my friends
on the road to October.

SMILE

Let the apple strudel light your way
to happier realms.

The world's been a sad place
a long time now.

You're going to have to do
what everyone else before you had to do —

you're going to have to smile
and go on.